A COMPANION GUIDE TO
RADICAL HOSPITALITY

Father Daniel Homan, OSB
and Lonni Collins Pratt

Robert B. Gibson

PARACLETE PRESS
BREWSTER, MASSACHUSETTS

2005 First printing

Copyright © 2005 by Paraclete Press, Inc.

10 9 8 7 6 5 4 3 2 1

ISBN 1-55725-461-3

Published by Paraclete Press
Brewster, Massachusetts
www.paracletepress.com

Printed in the United States of America

Contents

Contents

Introduction to This Guide

The *Companion Guide to Radical Hospitality* was developed for both individual and group use. Each chapter in this guide will develop the central theme in the corresponding chapter in *Radical Hospitality* and stimulate further reflection on the subject. A prayer is included that invokes God's presence, without which none of us can grasp the truth or embrace the healing that this book offers. The quotations from each chapter will enable you to discover significant points for discussion and reflection. As you read the book, look for other points that you may want to reflect on as well. The Scripture texts included at the end of each chapter will assist you or your class to further explore how the Bible is the foundation for each of the topics.

This guide will enable anyone who is concerned about hospitality to explore *Radical Hospitality* more beneficially. It is ideal for pastors, deacons, lay pastors, counselors, or other interested people to use in a small group Bible study, or retreat.

Introduction to *Radical Hospitality*

"If spirituality matters to you, you can't do spirituality
alone either. To really grow as a human being
you need other people" (p. ix).

Prayer for the Lesson
"God, grant us the ability to see how other people in
our lives are gifts from you and that they are as necessary
to our healing and well-being as the air we breathe.
In Jesus' name. Amen."

Truths from the Text
1) "Benedict wrote the *Rule* within the context of his
Christian faith, and so his teaching cannot be separated from
the teachings of Jesus. . . . A rule is nothing more than a set
of ideas to help you determine the kind of person you will be
. . ." (p. x). What shapes your life? Write a short list of
things that you do and think that shape your life.

2) "[H]ospitality was not about social graces but about
mutual reverence. Father Noel knew that spirituality is
about relationships. Every man, woman, and child bears to

us the presence of God" (p. xviii). What is your definition of hospitality? How does this present definition challenge that idea? Describe a time when another human being showed you God's presence without saying anything about God.

3) "Benedict tells us to offer an open heart, a stance of availability, and to look for God lurking in every single person who comes through the door" (p. xviii). Think of one person who has made himself or herself available to you. How did you experience God through this person? Think about one person whom you met unexpectedly in the last three days. How was God "lurking" in them?

4) "Unless we find a way to open ourselves to others, we will grow even more isolated and frightened. If we do not find and practice hospitality, we will grow increasingly hostile. . . . Jesus said to love your neighbor; hospitality is how" (p. xxii). When have you recently been fearful? Was your natural reaction to close yourself off from those around you? How might opening yourself up with another person be a way out of your fear? What risks do you take in opening up?

5) "Living life in a way that places a higher value on relationships and community than it does on commerce and productivity—this is counter to how most of us have been taught" (p. xxv). Is your life weighted more toward productivity or relationships?

Explain. Who is a role model in your life for each of these values?

6) "We hide out, isolate ourselves, and deny our natural need for others. We erroneously think we need safety the most. What we need most is acceptance. . . . We need to connect and feel the deep acceptance of another human being and that will make the world feel safer" (p. xxv). Reflect on the ways in which you "hide" from others and have denied your need to connect with those around you. When have you felt "safe" with another person? Share what happened.

Final Reflection Exercise
"It is a great loss if we greet every day with
clenched fists stuffed with our own devices. We
will never know what is out there waiting for us
if we don't extend an empty hand to the world and
wait for the wonder to happen" (p. xxxvii).

- R E F L E C T on how you typically start your day. Are you more of an open-handed or a "clenched-fist" person? Reflect on one day this week that would be typical for you.
- L I S T E N to what God may be saying to you about a choice you can make that will help you be more open to his moving in your day.

- I M A G I N E God coming into a situation where you have "clenched fists." How might he help you let go of your grip? How might others be a part of this process?
- C O M M I T yourself to acting on one thing that can help you change.

Further Scriptural Exploration

In the following passages, reflect on how God intervened in the lives of his people using strangers: Joseph and the Midianite traders (Genesis 37:17b–28); Ruth and Boaz (Ruth 2:1–10); the unexpected Samaritan (Luke 10:29–37); the parable with unexpected visitors (Matthew 25:31–46).

one The Taming of Hospitality

"We probably will never have to build a secret room in our homes to save the lives of people we don't know—but can we carve out a small place in our hearts for others? That is the true meaning of hospitality." (p. 13).

Prayer for the Lesson
God, You have sent Your Son and others into our lives to love us. Enlarge our lives so that we can make space for those whom You send into our daily experience. In Jesus' name. Amen.

Truths from the Text
1) "Somewhere, sometime, you were excluded. Remember what that was like. Some people live with the experience constantly" (p. 3). Reflect on a time when you were not chosen or accepted into a group. What happened? What did you feel at that time? What are your feelings now?

2) "The horror of September 11, 2001, did not create bigotry against Muslims; it incited existing bigotry. It fed a silently held bigotry already alive in a dark corner of our hearts. It

uncapped a quietly seething suspicion" (p. 8). Reflect on this assertion about bigotry toward Muslims in the aftermath of September 11th. Where in your life have you had to struggle with bigotry or suspicion of others? Share this with others.

3) "Hospitality has two meanings with most people today. It either refers to hotels or cruise ships, or it is connected to entertaining friends and family. . . . One model makes it an industry. . . . The other model relegates it to the domain of entertainment and housekeeping, generally considered women's work" (p. 10). How have these meanings shaped your understanding of hospitality? What are some of the flaws in these definitions?

4) "When I consider the stranger I am faced with my worst fears. I can't deny that I am afraid and that I don't even always like people" (p. 15). How does this sentiment reflect your own feelings?

5) "Hospitality is born in us when we are well loved by God and by others. Hospitality is the overflowing of a heart that has to share what it has received" (p. 20). Think of a recent moment where you experienced hospitality from God or another person. What happened? How did you react?

6) "Merely being nice to people does not fulfill the deep requirements of Benedictine hospitality. We must let the

person stir us; we must connect" (p. 21). What about this definition challenges you? Disturbs you? Directs you in a current situation?

Final Reflection Exercise
"God is experienced in the darkness in a way that is unique to darkness. And God in the dark makes the frightful thing less so. Fear chokes out love. We don't become people of love unless we have faced our fears" (p. 30).

- R E F L E C T on how times of darkness can enable us to discover the love of God. How does Psalm 23:4 encourage us to embrace the darkness and move through it with God?
- L I S T E N for how other Christians have found darkness to be a positive experience from which they emerged strengthened.
- I M A G I N E with God's help a time when you were in difficulty and believed that you were alone. How did God change that perception?
- C O M M I T yourself to being available this week to help someone who is struggling.

Further Scriptural Exploration:

Jesus was constantly making Himself available to people who were on the edge of Jewish society and were seen as a nuisance by many Jews. Reflect on how Jesus connected with and cared for the people in the following scriptural accounts: Luke 7:36–39, 44–50 (the notorious woman of sin); Luke 18:35–43 (the blind Jericho beggar); Luke 19:1–10 (the chief tax collector Zaccheus); John 9:1–12 (the blind man).

two Hospitality Begins Inside

Chapter Principle

"Here is the core of hospitality: May I know you better?
Will you come closer, please? No, it will not be easy,
but . . . your life depends on this saving stranger coming
to you and stretching your tight little heart" (p. 36).

Prayer for the Lesson

Dear God, warm our cold hearts so that they start
to expand and make room for those you would bring
into our lives. Free us from the constraints of fear and the
preoccupation with ourselves. In Jesus' name. Amen.

Truths from the Text

1) "Because hospitality always involves giving something of
ourselves to others, it is a spiritual practice. Spirituality is
about relationship. . . . [R]emembering that spirituality is about
relationships will bring us back to basics" (p. 34). Reflect on
one relationship that you treasure. What did you receive that
made the relationship valuable? What did you give?

2) "Genuine spirituality is not cozy, and seldom makes you
comfortable. It challenges, disturbs, unsettles, and leaves
you feeling like someone is at the center of your existence on

a major remodeling mission" (p. 35). How do you respond to the authors' assertion that genuine spiritual growth "challenges, disturbs, and unsettles . . ."? How is this assertion valid? What evidence do you have in your life that God has been on a "major remodeling mission"?

3) "Hospitality . . . is something you enter. It is an adventure that takes you where you never dreamed of going. It is not something you do, as much as it is someone you become. . . . This is how we grow more hospitable—by welcoming one person when the opportunity is given to you" (p. 38). Do you prefer the status quo predictability of life, or do you like the unfolding of an adventure to somewhere unknown? How does your life reflect both aspects?

4) "In most situations we get ourselves into trouble by what we do: adultery, lying, stealing, jealousy, and so on. Not so in hospitality: Our error comes through what we fail to do. . . . [W]e become less by what we omit doing" (p. 41). Where have you passed up the opportunities to be hospitable that have been presented to you recently? Why is this type of shortcoming particularly damaging to developing a ministry of hospitality?

5) "We fear bonding and we fear detachment, and we seldom know how to strike a healthy balance between them. . . . The need to belong and the need to be alone are both normal and

do not exclude the other" (p. 46). Do you see yourself as more of a bonding or a separate/detached person? Explain. Why does hospitality demand that we develop both aspects?

6) "The essence of hospitality is receiving the stranger while letting them remain a stranger. . . . We welcome them to be heard and understood, we accept what they choose to reveal of themselves, and we accept them if they reveal little or nothing" (p. 50). Think of a person who is a close friend. How does this relationship reflect the definition of hospitality? In terms of this definition, what is one thing you might do to be more hospitable?

Final Reflection Exercise:
"You and I, we can help the one in our path. That is enough.
Try to get this straight, that really is enough" (p. 42).

- R E F L E C T on what this tells you about hospitality. Why is this a significant challenge as well as a good focus?
- L I S T E N to God speaking to you through others about where you are being challenged in the call to hospitality.
- I M A G I N E that in six months your fellowship group is a more hospitable place. How will it need to change?
- C O M M I T yourself to cooperating with God this week as He places people in your path who need a moment of your time and energy.

Growing in hospitality is initially a matter of the heart and may seem like a huge task when we feel set in our ways of relating. But God is willing to mold and shape our inner heart attitudes if we ask. Hospitality starts in the heart. Here are a sampling of scriptural illustrations: Jeremiah and the good figs (Jeremiah 24:4–7); God's promise to restore Israel (Ezekiel 11:17–20); God's giving Israel a new heart (Ezekiel 36:24–27); staying connected to Jesus and His life (John 15:4–8).

three Welcoming the Other

Chapter Principle

"Let's consider what it means to be the 'other.' The other is the one who is not like me. She is the liberal if I am conservative, and rich if I am poor. . . . The other is the person from the neighborhood I avoid; the guy I don't want sitting next to me on the plane." (p. 63)

Prayer for the Lesson

God, we naturally gravitate toward those who are like us and turn from those who are different from us. Enable us to welcome strangers with the acceptance that You showed us when we were separated from You by our fallen nature. In Jesus' name we pray. Amen.

Truths from the Text

1) "We all tend to surround ourselves with people who agree with us on the vital issues, people who look like us, smell like us, have similar backgrounds, and hold similar convictions. It is natural to do this" (p. 64). If you could spend a day with three adults who are not family members, who would they be? How would these people be similar to you? How do your choices reflect the authors' premise?

2) "When we create a life surrounded by people just like ourselves, it is a very narrow life. We will not be challenged by such a life. We cave in on ourselves; our minds and spirits shrink to the pea-size of our world. . . . Letting ourselves believe that our experience constitutes normality . . . is delusional and dangerous" (p. 65). What about your life is stretching and forcing you to enter into the world and understanding of another? In what ways is your life predictable and based on your own set of realities? Would you characterize your world as narrow or broad? Reflect on this.

3) "[I]n relating to the person, we must offer them room to feel what they feel, rather than assuming that we know what they feel. Even if we think we have been through exactly the same experience ourselves, we cannot know what another is feeling" (p. 70). What risks does this manner of relating present? Think of a conversation you had recently with a person who was a stranger to you. Analyze your responses in light of the above description. How did you fare?

4) "When we hold tightly to a worldview in which our own experience is at the center, we live small lives. . . . [W]e can easily slip into suspicion, misunderstanding, and prejudice of strangers—those who do not meet our standard of 'normal'" (pp. 70-71). When have you recently been suspicious in a

relationship? How did your reaction cause you to misjudge or misinterpret the other person?

5) "Suspicion is one of the enemies of hospitality. Fear is at the core of suspicion. We are all starved for love, yet we are mostly unwilling to trust others to give us what we need" (p. 72). Think of two close friends. What events or incidents have enabled you to trust your friends? How did these incidents enable you to overcome your fear of being known and your fear of knowing the other person?

6) "When we place the great 'I' at the center of our universe, we give no value to anyone else. We make commodities of people, consuming them for our personal enrichment and happiness. It's common in our culture. The other's only purpose is what he or she can do for us" (p. 72). When have you misused a relationship and made a commodity of another person? When have you felt used by someone else? How was the great "I" at the center of these incidents?

Final Reflection Exercise

"At the root of many less-than-welcoming attitudes toward others is fear. If I am not at home in my own skin, enough to let someone else share my space, how will I ever be able to look on the stranger with anything like kindness and welcome?" (p. 76).

- R E F L E C T on how fear of others causes you to keep people out of your life. Be specific about one current example of this.
- L I S T E N when others share how fear has hindered the growth of healthy relationships. How can you identify with their examples?
- I M A G I N E that God intervened to free you from your fear in a certain relationship. How would that relationship change? Give a specific example of what you would do differently.
- C O M M I T yourself to allowing God to free you from fear in one relationship so that the relationship can mature.

Further Scriptural Exploration

Our attitude toward strangers is governed largely by either fear or compassion. When fear is predominant, self is at the center of our reactions. When compassion is reflected, God is seen in the response. How is this pattern reflected in the following Scriptures? Israel's treatment of foreigners (Deuteronomy 10:12–19); Herod's reaction to the Wise Men and their news (Matthew 2:1–4); Jesus and the centurion (Matthew 8:5–13); Peter receives the Gentiles (Acts 10:9–23).

four Cloister, Community, and Hospitality

Chapter Principle
"We need time alone (cloister), we need time with those closest to us (community), and we need to open ourselves to those who are not one of us (hospitality)." (p. 89)

Prayer for the Lesson
Almighty God, as you created us to be whole, balanced people, develop in us the ability to move between solitude, relationships with those near to us, and those strangers that you bring into our lives. In Jesus' name we pray. Amen.

Truths from the Text
1) "The hardest thing can be carving out time for silence. Our contemporary lives are hectic and noisy. We are driven by devices, and surrounded by machines. We have grown comfortable with the background noise. . . . It [noise] keeps life at a distance and also keeps us from noticing what is going on inside us" (pp. 90-91). What is your attitude toward silence? What role does it play in your life? What noises do you lean on in order to keep silence out?

2) "If you stay with solitude, you discover that this inner void is your friend. It is your true hunger. It has God's name on it. It tells you the truth about yourself, once you are able to push aside all the garbage that initially erupts out of it" (p. 92). Have you ever felt silence to be your friend? If so, describe when this happened. What do you truly hunger for? What are some of the distractions that you battle when you find moments of silence?

3) "Solitude . . . propels us outward and opens us up. It is from hours spent alone that a monk comes to cherish relationships. It is from the silence that he learns to listen. It is in the deep, empty place inside himself that the monk finds God" (p. 94). What do you learn in this passage about the role of silence that bothers you? Helps you? Appeals to you? Explain.

4) "Companions give us the support we need to go on. They provide the tenderness of friendship and are a source of stability, wisdom, and growth. We need other people. Some of our companions we choose, such as friends or a spouse. But we are born with a whole set of relationships, for better or worse" (p. 97). When recently did you experience your need for the support of others? What did another person supply that you needed and could not do for yourself?

5) "We need hospitality in those closest of relationships. Every now and then you get so tired that you just want to be with people who don't require an explanation. Family can be that" (pp. 99-100). What role does family play in your life? What do you like to do when you are with "people who don't need an explanation"?

6) "We also need others, including people who are not close to our heart of hearts. We need simpler, uncomplicated relationships with others. Hospitality expects that we share ourselves, some part of ourselves at least. . . . 'Benedictine spirituality is intent on the distribution of self for the sake of the other . . .'" (p. 104). Think about others who are not close to your "heart of hearts." Why are these people important to your wholeness? Why do you need them?

Final Reflection Exercise
"We become more available as the one 'in skin' for others as we move toward a healthy balance in our relationships. Balance gives us freedom, it eases anxieties, and it makes room in our lives. Cloister, community, and hospitality— they represent this balance. Enter each deeply" (p. 106).

• R E F L E C T on why each of these three elements brings balance. What happens if one if absent?

- **L I S T E N** to others and let God speak to you through them about where you have strengths and deficiencies in these three areas.
- **I M A G I N E** the one element that you find the most lacking. How might it look if God were to strengthen it?
- **C O M M I T** yourself to assessing and thanking God for how he has built up these three basic parts in your life.

Further Scriptural Exploration

In considering what makes up a balanced life, the following Scriptures are a small sampling of wisdom: cloister/silence (Psalm 4:4; Psalm 46:10, Mark 1:35); community/family (Proverbs 17:17, 18:24, Ecclesiastes 4:9-10); strangers (Leviticus 19:34, Hebrews 13:2, 1 Peter 4:9).

five Preparing a Table

Chapter Principle
"In genuine hospitality we work to make our entire existence a welcoming table, a place prepared for others to be at ease, to receive from us comfort and strength." (p. 109)

Prayer for the Lesson
God, transform our view of work from being something we do for ourselves to being something we undertake for you and for others you bring into our lives. In Jesus' name. Amen.

Truths from the Text:
1) "The lesson is that we must take seriously our receiving of others. Whether we are cooking a meal, mowing the grass, scouring the sinks, or painting a wall, we are preparing for the Sacred to come to us" (p. 111). What is your view of work? What is your motive in doing the various tasks associated with daily life? How can work enable you to care for another person and experience the presence of God?

2) "The deep meaning of hospitality involves our entrance into the mess of things; it means we run right into the chaos

if that is what it takes. If we do this, there is a slow, mysterious something that happens, transforming the riot into something good" (p. 113). How do you react when you become involved in a chaotic, disorganized situation? Where in your life has God brought order out of confusion? Where is there a chaotic situation in your life that needs your involvement?

3) "In Latin, the word *companion* literally means to 'break bread' together. No wonder the Eucharist has such power. It is founded in our food experience, and our earliest experience of that is associated with warmth and touching. Food is powerful. It says, 'You belong here.' It comforts" (p. 115). What was your experience of mealtimes growing up? In what way did you have a sense of belonging? Did you sense estrangement? How does the Eucharist communicate to you how God feels about you?

4) "Our ability to make room for others, and the joy we do or do not find in such activity, depends largely on our experience of being accepted or not. We build shelter for others because somewhere along the way someone sheltered us and thereby taught our hungry heart how to love" (pp. 117-18). Who in your childhood showed you acceptance? How did that person demonstrate that he or she loved you? How can this example help you relate to others?

5) "In human labor an astonishing thing happens: God shows up. As we prepare a place for others, something happens inside of us: We are prepared also. The Benedictine motto is 'Pray and work.' Benedictines consider work holy. Human labor is a reflection of divine work" (pp. 122-23). Describe your attitude toward work. Do you see it as a "God shows up" endeavor? Is it something you expect to do without His aid? How can you be more receptive to God in the work you do?

6) "The monks . . . have chosen to care for others on a daily basis just as they care for themselves. To do so is to be human. As we wash our bodies and fold our clothing and shovel the driveway, we indicate that we have accepted our role and life, as it exists. We are making peace with ourselves and all the others around us" (p. 125). What have you learned about the importance of attending to the details of daily life? How does attention to details reflect your care for others? What is your attitude toward details?

Final Reflection Exercise

"The most important work is preparing yourself to receive others. Only you know what you need to do to make that happen. Is there someone to forgive? . . . Is there a fear to abandon? . . . We all have weapons to lay down and battles to call off before we can open up our hearts. It is a stance of surrender that we are talking about. . . . Hospitality . . . is about the heart you make ready. Yours." (pp. 127-28).

- R E F L E C T on the assertion that we all have interior weapons and battles that keep us from hospitality. Where have you experienced the truth of this?
- L I S T E N to how God is getting your attention regarding one attitude that has kept you from being more open to others.
- I M A G I N E how your life would be if this attitude were healed.
- C O M M I T yourself to talking to someone you trust about what you see and about how God may be leading you.

Further Scriptural Exploration

In the following passages the theme of work is explored. Work is something we do in partnership with God. To do any task apart from God is to secularize it and empty it of its sacred presence. Psalm 127:1-2; 1 Corinthians 3:9, 12:6, 15:58; 1 Peter 4:11.

six Companionship and Intimacy

Chapter Principle
"Most of us will have intimate relationships, but we make a mistake if we think that intimacy is all we need. We also need companions, we need good fun, we need the brief and tender moment when a stranger stoops to collect the clutter that has dropped to the floor." (pp. 136-37)

Prayer for the Lesson
God, we were made to relate to others both in a vulnerable and in a casual manner. Help us to cherish both. Lead us in the relationships that you provide for us. In Jesus' name we pray. Amen.

Truths from the Text
1) "It is impossible to exaggerate the number of people who never feel heard, even by friends, family, or spouse. Being a person of hospitality involves getting out of myself for long enough periods that I can hear other people, really hear them, and pay attention to what they might need at this moment" (p. 131). When have you sensed recently that another person heard you? Describe what happened and

how you knew that you had connected with that person. When have you tried to communicate and were unsuccessful?

2) "Emulating someone is a good way to learn hospitality. Find a hospitable person and spend time with them. Listen to them. Do not look for methods or tips from them. Just be together and you will be astonished at what happens" (p. 132). Think about someone whom you consider a hospitable person. What qualities and actions reflect their openness and care toward you? How have you benefited from this relationship?

3) "Intimacy does not consist of a constant level of relating; instead, it simply happens when it needs to if people are open and able to enter the moment" (p. 137). Reflect on one relationship where you feel there are times of transparency between you and the other person. What were the events that enabled this to happen? What made you open to intimacy? How has the relationship flowed between moments of vulnerability and normal life?

4) "We have lost completely the awareness that relationships come in degrees. We don't know how to move from casual to intimate and back again. We have forgotten that we ought to pour ourselves out sometimes, and hold back at other times. . . . Hospitality is not a call to unquestioning intimacy with the whole world" (p. 139). How does this statement

speak to you about the relationships in your life? In what ways do you move from casual to intimate?

5) "When we confuse intimacy with sexual relations, we imply that sex is the only means to closeness. . . . Dozens of relationships involve intimacy, including parental and family ones. To make intimacy explicitly sexual is to suggest that these closest relationships are less than intimate. When I experience genuine intimacy, I know to the bone that I am not alone" (pp. 140-41.) How does the world equate sex with true intimacy? How does the above statement expose this myth? What do you learn in this statement about genuine intimacy?

6) "Intimacy happened in America when every American we knew was sitting in front of a television watching the events of September 11 unfold. . . . We experienced a brief period of knowing we are part of one another and we belong to each other. That was an experience of intimacy we shared with strangers, the people next door, and our best friends" (p. 144.) In what way did September 11 create an intimate moment for you? Why was it intimate? What other event brought you into intimacy with both friends and strangers? Describe what happened.

Final Reflection Exercise

"But that's how intimacy works. It happens when we least expect it, and it shows up in odd situations between strangers. It makes strangers into brothers and sisters. It flares up and gives us an emotional rush of acceptance and belonging and being known, and then it ebbs away . . ." (p. 147).

- R E F L E C T on an intimate moment that occurred in your life recently. How was the moment unexpected? How was it risky? How did you feel? Why was it intimate?

- L I S T E N to how God is involved in orchestrating these unexpected moments.

- I M A G I N E that you were free of fear or reluctance to enter into an intimate moment of sharing. What would you be like?

- C O M M I T yourself to embracing the relationships that come to you this week.

Further Scriptural Exploration

Intimate relationships are ones in which God is involved as we relate both directly to Him and to others who become part of our lives. In the following scriptural stories, what makes for intimacy? God's conversation with Moses (Exodus

3:4–12); Naomi's conversation with Ruth (Ruth 1:8–18); Jonathan and David (1 Samuel 20:1–4, 41-42); Saul on the Damascus Road (Acts 9:1–9); the early church's intimacy with Jesus (1 John 1:1–4).

seven The Making of a Heart—
It's Not Easy to Love

Chapter Principle

"There is always the real you. The one with the
potential. The one you dream of becoming. The one
you are in your best moments. As we grow spiritually,
we recover this original identity and shed the
many layers of the false self." (p. 157)

Prayer for the Lesson

God, continue your work of restoration in me so that
I will move through difficulties to embrace not only
times of suffering, but also live out of gratitude,
joy, and courage. In Jesus' name. Amen.

Truth From the Text

1) "You are becoming something. You are becoming more
patient, more loving, more angry, more selfish—there is
some fundamental person at the root of it all. It may be a
person of love, or a person of selfish indifference. Every day
we make choices that take us toward becoming one or the
other" (pp. 157-58). Look back over the last twenty-four
hours. How do you see persons, both loving and selfish,

coming through the events of your life? What choices were significant in encouraging you to be more loving?

2) "Our ability to accept others begins with whether or not we are in touch with our dark side. As we have said, monks live with themselves without blinking at the dark side, and this is what allows them to be as accepting as they are. They are able to accept strangers without expecting them to be perfect" (p. 158). Reflect on how your ability to accept others is related to their knowing your dark side. Why is knowing one's dark side an asset both in living life and relating to others?

3) "Gratitude is an appropriate response once you know who you really are. Gratitude for all the grace that overlooks the worst, while moving you toward your original best self" (p. 159). When have you most recently experienced gratitude in your life? In looking at times when you were grateful, how did that response flow out of a sense of your flaws or a sense of receiving something you did not deserve?

4) "Gratitude is at the center of a hospitable heart. It keeps everything in perspective. Often we allow day after gifted day to come and go without one sigh of gratitude for the beauty of it all. We don't slow our breath to hear the song of the wind, or taste the miracle of an apple. . . . What an arrogant life we lead" (p. 162). Reflect on your last twenty-four

hours and list all the "gifted" moments that occurred in your day. In what ways can you recognize your arrogance? How does gratitude contrast with arrogance?

5) "You really cannot make it happen; gratitude, like faith, is given to you. . . . Gratitude happens most often during suffering, loss, and other really hard stuff. It is the leading edge of joy. It happens when the big reality hits you. You have no more right to be loved than anyone else" (p. 163). How do you respond to the authors' assertion that gratitude grows out of hardship? How is the transition from suffering to gratitude to joy reflected in the life of someone you have admired?

6) "Anxiety makes you ready for gratitude. So does having enough courage not to dull the anxiety with alcohol, or spending, or eating, or whatever your usual escape might be. Shut the door, experience the anxiety, and you are ready for gratitude. . . . Try to force gratitude and you end up with guilt instead" (p. 163). What issues in your life are causing you to be anxious? How would you normally try to dull this anxiety? Practically, what might it mean to "shut the door and experience the anxiety" in one area of your life?

7) "What is the secret of people who seem always to feel grateful without being prompted . . . ? The secret is, these people have courage. . . . Courage takes us past thinking and

talking about hospitality into the realm of the will. Courage is the power of the heart, and it resides not in the emotion, but in the will and the power to choose" (pp. 166-67). How would you define courage in the life of someone you admire? How did they act courageously? Why does courage come down to a choice and not an emotion? Where in your life do you need courage?

Final Reflection Exercise

"The difficult person comes with a mountain of emotion attached. The emotion itself can become the center of any relating that happens. We are not doing the person any good if we become caught up in their emotion and negativity. If we center down into the quiet in our hearts, we can hear what is really happening. . . . When you are conscious of living every second gathered before the Divine you just do not rattle easily" (p. 170).

- R E F L E C T on what makes a person you know difficult. How do that person's emotions affect you?
- L I S T E N to how you can respond to that person differently by not getting hooked into their emotions.
- I M A G I N E that you are encountering that difficult person and you are spiritually prepared. How will you be different?

• C O M M I T yourself to acting differently next time you
encounter a difficult person.

Further Scriptural Exploration

In the following stories from the life of Christ, reflect on how
He handled difficult people. He invariably responded with a
poise and wisdom that only God could give. He was not
caught up in the emotional difficulties that accompanied
each situation. Jesus and a mother's request (Matthew
20:20–28); Peter's news of the crowds (Mark 1:35–39); the
Pharisees confront Jesus about the adulterous woman (John
8:1–11); Jesus responds to Martha (Luke 10:38–42, John 11:
17–27).

eight Making Room for Yourself

Chapter Principle
"Denying what we really and truly need, in some misunderstood notion about being hospitable toward others, or loving with others, is simply bad for you. You need time to yourself. You need respect" (p. 179).

Prayer for the Lesson
Dear God, though your Son was the servant of us all, He would withdraw from humanity so that He could seek your presence, will, and wisdom. Teach us about maintaining our own set of necessary boundaries. In Jesus' name. Amen.

Truths from the Text
1) "The family he came from had not taught him to respect other people or to insist that others respect you. The real meaning of *boundaries* is the insistence that I will not be violated by your selfishness" (p. 175). As you grew up, how did you learn about respecting the conversations, needs, or wishes of other people in your family? Where were the boundaries?

2) "Being a person with strong and wise boundaries does not make you selfish. It is refusing to let others have boundaries that makes you selfish; it is insisting that others must make

you the center of their lives that is selfish" (pp. 178-79). When have you recently crossed over the boundary line of another person? When has another person crossed your boundaries? Describe each situation and how you responded.

3) "Boundaries do not exclude the other; in fact, if you become a person with actual boundaries, you are better able to give to other people because you do not feel diminished by it. Giving is a joy because you want to give, and not because someone has manipulated you and you gave in" (p. 179). What kind of boundaries have you set for yourself? How have they proven helpful to you? Cite a specific example of a necessary boundary that you maintain.

4) "You're also distinctive. You must remain who you are, and allow yourself to grow more yourself every day. Hospitality will help that happen, . . . but you must remain freely yourself. If you lose your distinctiveness, the world has lost something it will never see again—you" (pp. 184-85). Make a short list of what is distinctive about you. What are you doing to maintain your distinctiveness and follow your loves? What has threatened your distinctiveness?

5) "The part of us that we give to others, to the stranger you might say, is our outer self. . . . With the outer self we give attention. We listen. We offer genuine concern. . . . We

appreciate the person, and give them something of ourselves, without expecting them to become a friend. We don't necessarily share secrets, inner feelings, dreams, or ambitions and passions" (p. 185). Reflect on both your outer and inner self. In what ways over the last week have you seen the contrast between the two? What can you learn from the above quote about offering the one and protecting the other?

6) "It can be emotionally draining to give yourself to someone who has the neediness of a child. These are the people who are most likely to push against your boundaries, and they rarely have boundaries of their own. They are also the most in need of a simple gesture of acceptance" (pp. 186-87). When have you attempted to befriend another person who had many needs and found yourself drained after each encounter? How did this person push against your boundaries? How did you respond? What simple gesture of acceptance did you offer, or what might have you offered?

Final Reflection Exercise
"Opening up to others does not mean you let someone trample all over you. . . . It does not mean you cease to take care of yourself or do what you need to do to remain emotionally, physically, and spiritually healthy. We can give simple kindness without losing ourselves" (p. 189).

- R E F L E C T on what it means to be available to others, having a healthy set of boundaries.
- L I S T E N for ways in which you need to reach out and still nurture those parts of your life that are distinctive and unique to your personality.
- I M A G I N E yourself six months from now. What is one way in which you hope to be more open and one thing you can do to develop that gift?
- C O M M I T yourself to doing one thing that will help you grow in both your outward and inner self.

Further Scriptural Exploration

Though He was fully God, Jesus was also fully human. The following Gospel accounts reflect some of His boundaries. His early healing ministry (Mark 1:29–34); His commitment to keep the Passover (Luke 22:7–16); reacting to the temple's misuse (John 2:13–22); Jesus' physical limits (John 4:4–7).

nine Being a Companion Through the Hurt

Chapter Principle

"We don't have to have all the answers to companion the hurting. Actually people who try to offer answers are not particularly comforting. . . . Forget answers. Be available. Be available with eyes wide open. Know it is going to interrupt your well-planned life." (p. 206)

Prayer for the Lesson

Dear God, Your Son, Jesus, made Himself available in the upper room to wash the feet of His followers. He commanded us to follow His example. Teach us to respond to the needs that occur in our daily lives. In Your name we pray. Amen.

Truths from the Text

1) "We don't deal with the hard realities, such as beautiful children suffering, unless we are forced to. We get through life with some peace of mind by not looking at the hungry children, the dying children, the bombed children. . . . It takes a whole lot of courage to do otherwise" (p. 192). How do you respond when you are confronted with the realities of

suffering? Do you seek peace by avoiding an awareness of suffering, or have you found peace in the midst of suffering? Apply this to a stressful situation in your family or among your friends.

2) "'I don't know how I would have survived without Linda. . . . She became the face of God to me when God seemed gone. I could not find a way to pray, or believe in a good God. I could not get past the anger and doubt, but I could hold onto this woman. . . . I didn't have to give back anything. . . . It was the hardest time I've ever known . . . '" (p. 195). How does this testimony speak to you about the role of others in times of suffering? How can you identify with the woman who gave this testimony?

3) "When people are bent over with the weight of suffering, they need from us only our presence. If we give them that, truly give them that, we become for them the presence of God in a most tangible way. That is hospitality. . . . Few of us will ever be involved in such a life-shattering situation. But we can be present in everyday ways to those who hurt and those who are shunned. We can make a pot of chili . . . offer to baby-sit . . ." (p. 196). How is hospitality described in these sentences? How do we disqualify ourselves when we consider ourselves unable to be of assistance? How has someone cared for you by doing simple things that mattered?

4) "You can't engage with human pain and remain unchanged. But that is the beauty of it. It will cost you everything and you will gain everything. . . . God is present in the awful thing—not as its origin, but as the One who even in the most skin-crawling and torturous of events, offers the miraculous possibility of healing and a new beginning" (p. 197). What challenge does suffering present to all of us? Where have you experienced suffering as a transforming and enriching influence in your life? How does this picture of God instruct and challenge the image of God that you know?

5) "Most people can simplify life by just being honest with themselves and deciding what matters most. . . . [M]aking promises and keeping promises will free us to be more open to others. Commitment brings with it a great deal of freedom because, by its nature, it closes down options. We have become a people of too many options" (p. 205). List the seven things you do that matter most to you. Where can you simplify this list? What promises have you made that you need to keep? How do you react to the statement, "Commitment brings with it a great deal of freedom"?

6) "Commitment means we are going to show up tomorrow for work and will keep the same spouse we live with today. The more committed we are to our family, friends, and our convictions, the more free we become to be open to others.

Commitment settles us down. . . . By closing up some options, commitment frees you to live in peace with yourself. It quiets the struggles" (pp. 205-206). What basic commitments have you made? How have they brought you peace? How have they brought you freedom? Are you struggling inwardly? What commitment are you being asked to make?

Final Reflection Exercise

"The stranger is a lot like God, after all. God is constantly disrupting our best plans, God shows up when it is less than convenient, God is present no matter what we do to shoo him off. How we live with these strangers who keep messing up our plans will determine the future for all of us" (p. 206).

- R E F L E C T on how God has shown up as the unexpected stranger in your life. Where has He interrupted your plans?
- L I S T E N to others when they talk about the goodness and love of God that arrived in unforeseen situations.
- I M A G I N E that God is calling you to let Him enter some tightly controlled area or relationship in your life. What would it be?
- C O M M I T yourself to following God's leading in a new direction that you would not otherwise have chosen.

Further Scriptural Exploration:
We live in a world that trumpets the virtues of unbridled freedom and is unaware that the true doorway to freedom is making commitments to doing the will of God. Explore some of the commitments made in the calls God extended to His people in Scripture: the call of Abraham (Genesis 12:1–4); the call of Moses (Exodus 3:4–12); Jesus calls His disciples (Matthew 28:16–20, John 21:15–19, Acts 26:12–18).

ten Listening: The Deep Truth of Hospitality

Chapter Principle

"Listen, the ancient monk [St. Benedict] tells us, listen.
It will break your heart, but it will also give you a heart.
And it will give you more—it will give you life.
Only Love is strong enough to hold all the pain in
the world. Love will listen." (p. 213)

Prayer for the Lesson

Dear God, Your Son came to the earth and sought to
transform His followers into people who could hear.
Touch our hearts and ears so that we might listen deeply to
those who are around us. In Jesus' name we pray. Amen.

Truths from the Text

1) "Listening, as Benedict understood it, is a special kind of
deep attentiveness to all of life. Benedict understood that we
can live in ways that either dull or sharpen this attentiveness"
(p. 209). Who in your life is a good listener? How have you
experienced this gift? What can you do to sharpen this skill?

2) "When we learn to listen, we will hear screams, and the
sound of another's suffering changes everything. It unsettles
us, breaks apart our comfort, and makes us choose a side.

We become less human when we decide to do nothing once we have heard the screams. . . . It isn't easy to stay open. God knows it isn't easy" (p. 212). How can you identify with this description of how pain affects us? How have you sensed God's presence in the midst of pain? How are you trying to stay connected to a person who is hurting?

3) "That's how you feel when someone listens to you: Real. . . . When a human being isn't heard, when all that is special to a child is ignored . . . that person is in grave danger of becoming less than they were made for" (p. 215). When you were growing up, who was the listening person in your life? How did you know you were being heard? How did someone else's listening make you feel "real"?

4) "Listening is the power of hospitality; it is what makes hospitality the lifegiving thing it is. When you listen, you get past yourself, too. . . . In the listening stance, the focus switches from the self to the other" (pp. 215-16). Think about a time when you listened well. What did you do to get "past yourself"?

5) "[W]hile the people we listen to benefit, in the end we are the ones transformed. Benedict doesn't call us to listen on the surface. He wants us to listen with the ears of the soul. Listen way down deep. You know the place; it's the same place that weeps at the sight of a newborn, the same place that falls silent at the edge of a mountain . . ." (p. 220). How is

superficial listening far easier compared to listening with the "ears of the soul"? Has there been a time when another's listening ability enriched your life? Describe what happened.

6) "Listening is important because it forms bonds between people and reinforces self-worth. People feel better when they have been listened to. . . . By really hearing someone, we come to realize that we never perfectly understand anyone. That realization helps us drop the unrealistic expectation that anyone will ever completely understand us" (p. 221). List the benefits of listening well. Which ones can you most readily relate to? Which ones are more challenging to you? Why?

Final Reflection Exercise

"But we can help each other climb the difficult stairs of our lives; we can help each other when moving under our own steam just is not going to happen. We can . . . look right into one another's eyes. We can help each other make it to places that have been closed to us" (p. 229).

- R E F L E C T on a time when you couldn't make it "under your own steam." What happened? Who was there for you?
- L I S T E N for how God has provided people for needy friends of yours. Can you start to see how God has been more present to you than you might have thought?

- I M A G I N E you were to grow in one phase of your listening ability. What would happen?
- C O M M I T yourself to cooperating with God by becoming a better listener.

Further Scripture Exploration

The Scriptures are clear that listening is an active word. God is a God who hears the sighs of our souls and the words of our lips. Reflect on how listening happens in the following scriptural accounts: Moses at the burning bush (Exodus 3:7–20); Jesus with the woman at the well (John 4:15–19); our summons to listen (Matthew 13:16–23, 17:5; James 1:19), also Isaiah 65:24.

About Paraclete Press

Who We Are

Paraclete Press is an ecumenical publisher of books on Christian spirituality for people of all denominations and backgrounds.

We publish books that represent the wide spectrum of Christian belief and practice—Catholic, Orthodox, and Protestant.

We market our books primarily through booksellers; we are what is called a "trade" publisher, which means that we like it best when readers buy our books from booksellers, our partners in successfully reaching as wide an audience as possible.

We are uniquely positioned in the marketplace without connection to a large corporation or conglomerate and with informal relationships to many branches and denominations of faith, rather than a formal relationship to any single one. We focus on publishing a diversity of thoughts and perspectives—the fruit of our diversity as a company.

What We Are Doing

Paraclete Press is publishing books that show the diversity and depth of what it means to be Christian. We publish books that reflect the Christian experience across many cultures, time periods, and houses of worship.

We publish books about spiritual practice, history, ideas, customs, and rituals, and books that nourish the vibrant life of the church.

We have several different series of books within Paraclete Press, including the bestselling Living Library series of modernized classic texts, A Voice from the Monastery—giving voice to men and women monastics on what it means to live a spiritual life today, and Many Mansions—for exploring the riches of the world's religious traditions and discovering how other faiths inform Christian thought and practice.

Learn more about us at our Web site:
www.paracletepress.com, or call us toll-free at
1-800-451-5006.

Also Available for Small Group Study:

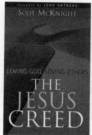

THE JESUS CREED
Scot McKnight
350 pages, ISBN: 1-55725-400-1
$16.95, Trade Paper

When an expert in the law asked Jesus for the greatest commandment, Jesus responded with the *Shema,* the ancient Jewish creed that commands Israel to love God with heart, soul, mind, and strength. But the next part of Jesus' answer would change the course of history. Jesus amended the *Shema,* giving his followers a new creed for life: to love God with heart, soul, mind, and strength, but also to love others as themselves.

"An excellent introduction to Christian spirituality. Its pages glow with compassion, generosity and the invitation to understand what was important to Jesus and what is crucial for Christianity."
—*Publishers Weekly*

A COMPANION GUIDE TO *THE JESUS CREED*
Scot McKnight

(Used by more than 1000 churches in 2004/2005!)

80 pages, ISBN: 1-55725-412-5
$5.95, Trade Paper

This *Companion Guide* enables the reader to anchor the lessons of *The Jesus Creed* into the depths of one's heart. Each day's *Guide* applies the fundamental spiritual formation principle of each chapter in *The Jesus Creed,* and then encourages us to dig deeper in the Gospels to learn more about how *The Jesus Creed* shaped the life of Jesus and all those around him.

Available from most booksellers or through Paraclete Press: www.paracletepress.com; 1-800-451-5006. Try your local bookstore first.